ZLATAN STYLE
The funniest Zlatan Ibrahimovic quotes!

About the author

Gordon Law is a freelance journalist and editor who has previously covered football for the *South London Press*, the *Premier League*, *Virgin Media* and a number of English national newspapers and magazines. He has also written several books on the beautiful game.

Also available to buy

ZLATAN STYLE

The funniest Zlatan Ibrahimovic quotes!

by Gordon Law

gordonlawauthor@yahoo.com

Printed in the United States of America
ISBN-13: 978-1545175644
ISBN-10: 1545175640

Photos courtesy of: Herbert Kratky/Shutterstock.com; Vlad1988/
Shutterstock.com; Paolo Bona/Shutterstock.com; Maxisport/
Shutterstock.com; katatonia82/Shutterstock.com; Paolo Bona/
Shutterstock.com; A_Lesik/Shutterstock.com; Christian
Bertrand/Shutterstock.com; Dziurek/Shutterstock.com

Contents

Introduction   6

Zlatan... on Zlatan   9

Others... on Zlatan   95

Zlatan fact file   111

Introduction

There are few footballers in the world that have ever provided as much entertainment on the pitch as they have done off it like Zlatan Ibrahimovic has.

The Swedish striker has been a prolific scorer – with a wonderful knack of netting spectacular goals – for each of the major European clubs he has played for during a trophy-laden career.

As one of the game's greatest personalities, he's rarely lost for words too, with his one-liners as notable as his wonder strikes.

Oozing with an incredible amount of confidence and belief, a very self-aware Zlatan loves to boast about his performances. And he's a cocksure, egotistical figure who regularly refers to himself in the third person.

The maverick Zlatan once claimed he was Jesus to inspire Paris Saint-Germain to the Ligue 1 title and has even compared himself to the great Muhammad Ali.

His hilarious outbursts make him one of the funniest sports stars around, and whether it's ridiculing teammates, opponents or even journalists, you can't help but laugh.

Zlatan has a darker side too and listening to him take down reporters or fellow pros in his own bombast way, especially his old Barcelona manager Pep Guardiola, is also amusing.

Zlatan's most ludicrous quips and quotes can be found here in this unique collection of 'Zlatanisms'. I hope you enjoy it!

Gordon Law

ZLATAN STYLE

Zlatan... on Zlatan

"Swedish style? No. Yugoslavian style? Of course not. It has to be Zlatan style."

The forward pays little attention to his mixed heritage when it comes to discussing his game

"Thank you, but to finish second is like finishing last. On that list I would have been number one, two, three, four and five, with due respect to the others."

Zlatan comes in behind tennis legend Bjorn Borg in a national poll for the top 150 Swedes of all time

"He [Giorgio Chiellini] tried to provoke me with a cowardly tackle from behind. I went down in a lot of pain but didn't say anything. I took my revenge after the final whistle, grabbing his head and dragging him along like a disobedient dog. I could see Chiellini was scared. 'You wanted to fight. So how come you're sh*tting yourself now?' I hissed before heading off to the changing room."

Zlatan takes no prisoners

Reporter: "What superpowers would you like to possess?"

Zlatan: "I already have them all."

"The first time I saw myself in a football video game I was super-excited. To see yourself in FIFA – wow! But don't be fooled – I am better in reality!"

Maybe the programmers have it wrong?

Reporter: "Was your new haircut in the World Cup inspired by Magnus Hedman?"

Zlatan: "No, I just went in and cut my hair and this is what I looked like when I came out."

"I will strike like lightning in Allsvenskan [the Swedish first division]."

On Malmo FF's return to the elite league

"Whatever, whatever, whatever. I don't need the money. I'm doing it because it's fun. These projects are fun to work with. It's new adventures for me. When I'm doing well and you feel a sting from it, then I'm enjoying myself even more... It's the same as when I'm playing football – I get an extra kick out of it if it hurts you. That's the best feeling."

Zlatan hits out at a reporter who queried his various projects outside the game

"You might have expected [Pep] Guardiola to say a few words in response, but he's a spineless coward."

He doesn't hold back on his old manager

"People trash talk me. I've heard so much sh*t over the years: 'F*cking gypsy', stuff about my mum – all that stuff. I retaliate with my body, not with words."

The frontman gives it to all the haters

Presenter: "Lionel Messi?"

Zlatan: "Fantastic."

Presenter: "Cristiano Ronaldo?"

Zlatan: "Good."

Presenter: "Zlatan Ibrahimovic?"

Zlatan: "Wow."

The striker is asked in a TV interview to describe star footballers in one word

"[Oguchi] Onyewu resembled a heavyweight boxer. He was nearly 6ft 5in and weighed over 15 stone, but he couldn't handle me."

Zlatan broke a rib during a scrap with his former AC Milan teammate

"I didn't injure you on purpose and you know that. If you accuse me again I'll break both your legs, and that time it will be on purpose."

The Swede threatens Rafael van der Vaart after the Dutch midfielder claimed he intentionally tried to injure him during an international with Holland

Zlatan goes on the attack for Manchester United against Zorya Luhansk in the Europa League.

"I came to the Premier League and everyone thought it would not be possible but, like always, I make them eat their balls. It gives me a lot of energy, trust me, because they get paid to talk sh*t and I get paid to play with my feet. That's how I enjoy it."

Newly arrived at Manchester United, Zlatan is happy to prove the critics wrong

"Oh, le meme… nose."

The Swede notices a female supporter with a similar hooter to him, but comically fails to remember the French word (it's 'nez')

"Become a coach? Impossible. Because during the match I'd slap at least two players and after the match, eight."

Zlatan admits he hasn't got the discipline to be a football manager

"I don't need the Ballon d'Or to know I'm the best. It matters more to some players."

The striker plays down the significance of the game's greatest individual award that he hasn't won

"I can play in the 11 positions because a good player can play anywhere on the pitch."

It's Mr Versatile

Reporter: "How does it feel to score with your wrong foot?"

Zlatan: "There is no wrong foot."

The frontman scored with his supposed weaker left foot in PSG's 4-0 win at Bayer Leverkusen in the Champions League

"Hey @MATUIDIBlaise I saw your goal last night. Magnifique. You must have been watching Zlatan in training."

Zlatan tweeted his PSG teammate Blaise Matuidi after he netted an acrobatic volley for France in a friendly against Holland

"I don't need a scary nickname. You just have to watch me to feel scared."

When asked why he didn't have a scary name, like Edinson Cavani (El Matador) or Radamel Falcao (El Tigre)

"I like [Mario] Balotelli: he's even crazier than me. He can score a winner, then set fire to the hotel."

He refers to the incident where the Italian caused a fire by setting off fireworks

"Nothing. She already has Zlatan."

When asked what he bought his future wife for her engagement present

"You were born as the one you are. I mean destiny, yes there is destiny. Some things are made by hard work, but quality you don't learn. Quality you are born with."

Zlatan on being born a star talent

"It was a joke. The cops laughed, but a photographer appeared and snapped a photo. Idiot that I was, I put on a huge grin. You can imagine what happened next."

On the incident where he and some friends imitated police officers and stopped a sex worker and a possible client in Malmo

"We were looking through his playlist in the dressing room – there was lots of Justin Bieber, Jonas Brothers and Selena Gomez. We were expecting some cool English rock bands and hip hop. It is nice to know that even David Beckham doesn't have good taste in everything."

Zlatan on his not-so-cool teammate Becks

Dutch reporter: "Can you describe 'Zlatan'? A lot of Dutch people don't understand?"

Zlatan: "I've never heard this question before, I think it's only you who doesn't understand."

Zlatan battles for the ball against Austria's Julian Baumgartlinger while playing for Sweden in a Euro 2004 qualifier.

Photo: Herbert Kratky/Shutterstock.com

"Today at training, journalists even started talking to me on the field, which is not normal. They shouldn't be allowed. I think France is not used to having someone in their country who is of my level."

Even the national media is in awe of Paris Saint-Germain's new signing

"I would have killed for Jose Mourinho, for the motivation he gave me and for how he used to stimulate me."

The player is prepared to go to extreme measures for his old boss

"Football is no longer burning inside me like back in the old days. It even takes a great deal of effort for me to play football with my kids in the garden – I now leave it to the babysitter."

Zlatan is happy to be substituted by the nanny in the twilight of his career

Q: "Is there anything in the world that could stop you from becoming no.1 in the world?"

A: "An injury."

"When my Italian teacher kicked me out of the lesson I said, 'I don't give a damn about you. I'll learn it when I become a pro in Italy'."

Zlatan was always confident he'd succeed

"I would love to play at the European Championship in France. I have played there for four years. I have put Sweden on the world map and now I have put France on the world map too."

Zlatan claims that Sweden and France are well known because of him

"I won't be the King of Manchester. I will be the God of Manchester."

A response to Eric Cantona who said: "There can only be one king in Manchester. You can be the prince if you want to"

"I'm still here doing what I have to do and doing it better and better. I'm like a fine wine that gets better with age."

Zlatan is confident about still producing the goods despite turning 34

Q: "How good is it to be able to walk in to a car outlet and be able to buy any car you want?"

A: "You'll have to get used to it."

"Now I am here [at PSG], I think the people in Paris will have something else to see besides the Mona Lisa."

Zlatan is the main attraction in town

"Arsene Wenger gave me the famous red and white jersey – the No.9 shirt with Ibrahimovic on it – and I was so pleased I even posed for a picture wearing it. He never actually made me a serious offer. It was more, 'I want to see how good you are, what kind of player you are. Have a trial'. I couldn't believe it. I was like, 'No way, Zlatan doesn't do auditions'."

He could have been a Gunners player

"I don't give a sh*t who wins, I'm going on holiday."

When asked who he thinks would win Euro 2012 after Sweden were knocked out

"They said they were going to send me to retirement. I sent their whole nation into retirement."

On scoring to take Sweden to victory in their Euro 2016 play-off against Denmark

"Absolutely not. I have ordered a plane. It is much faster."

Zlatan on rumours he had bought a Porsche

"I came here as a 35-year-old. Everybody thought I was in a wheelchair. What happened? The lion is still alive and that's the way it is."

On his first season in the Premier League

Zlatan bears down on the Shakhtar Donetsk goal for Paris Saint-Germain in the Champions League.

"People have the image of me that I'm a bad boy; I'm this and I'm that. People are curious: 'How is this Zlatan?' I'm a family guy. I'm taking care of my family, but when I come on the pitch I'm a lion. That's the big difference. I don't believe I'm arrogant in the way that people think. I'm confident. I believe in myself. That's not being arrogant. That's something I believe is an individual strength in the human being. I have confidence and I believe in myself. I have a vision and I do everything. I work hard for it. I don't believe that's arrogant."

Zlatan makes clear to Man United fans that his confidence is not arrogance

"For the moment, I will not be at PSG next season. I still have a month-and-a-half left here. If they replace the Eiffel Tower with a statue of me, then I will stay."

He issues an interesting ultimatum to Paris Saint-Germain

"Mourinho would become a guy I was basically willing to die for."

Zlatan really does adore Jose Mourinho

"An injured Zlatan is a pretty serious thing for any team."

Playing without the Swedish striker would hurt any side

"I like fireworks too, but I set them off in gardens or kebab stands. I never set fire to my own house."

Referring to Mario Balotelli unleashing a firework ahead of the Manchester derby

"When you buy me, you are buying a Ferrari. If you drive a Ferrari you put premium petrol in the tank, you hit the motorway and you step on the gas. [Pep] Guardiola filled up with diesel and took a spin in the countryside. He should have bought a Fiat."

Zlatan criticises Guardiola on how he was used at Barcelona

"There are a few moments I will see on the internet when I retire and I'll tell myself they're amazing. I'll ask myself how even I could have achieved such feats."

Zlatan on retiring

"We're looking for an apartment in Paris. If we don't find anything, then I'll probably just buy the hotel."

Zlatan on relocating his family after joining Paris Saint-Germain

"You can't coach brilliance like that."

On his amazing 30-yard overhead kick goal for Sweden against England in 2012

"Jose Mourinho is a big star. The first time he met my partner he said, 'Helena, you have one mission. Feed Zlatan, let him sleep, keep him happy'. That guy says whatever he wants. I like him."

On his bromance with Mourinho

"The Barca players were like schoolboys, following the coach blindly. Whereas I was used to asking, 'Why should we?'"

The forward explains what it was like to play at Barcelona

"I can't help but laugh at how perfect I am."

Zlatan is as modest as ever

Reporter: "You've got some scars on your face, Zlatan. What has happened?"

Zlatan: "Well... I don't know... You'll have to ask your wife about that."

Agent Anders Carlsson: "Southampton... Southampton is interested."

Zlatan: "What the f*ck! Southampton! Is that my level? Southampton!"

Unsettled at Ajax, Zlatan asks his agent if any clubs offered him a way out

"You can't be a clown all the time."

Zlatan on growing up after five months at Ajax

Zlatan shows his acrobatic side while playing for Inter Milan.

"Hi @Twitter. For tomorrow Zlatan needs more than 140 characters. Please change rules for Zlatan."

He tweeted this ahead of a Q&A on social media. The following are some of his best replies to fan questions...

"There are 2 things Zlatan cannot do @at_sunshine. One is be predictable. The other is a step-under. But Zlatan is practising. #DareToZlatan."

"Dear @EdgleyLFC. Daring to Zlatan is easy. Start by trying moves that can't be done. Keep trying until you are Zlatan. #DareToZlatan."

"Dear @ArmouredGuy, a wise man once said, surprising your opponent is the key to surprising them. That wise man was Zlatan. #DareToZlatan"

"Hi @Greg_douglass, failure is the first step to success. The second step is growing a ponytail. #DaretoZlatan."

"@AAlasfoor10 Zlatan's favourite stadium is the one with grass and two goals. Every stadium is a potential stage. #DareToZlatan."

"Am I mad @bailofwz? Would a sane man try a 32 yard overhead kick in an international match?"

"A World Cup without me is nothing to watch, so it is not worth waiting for the World Cup."

Zlatan in bullish mood after Sweden missed out on qualification for the 2014 contest

Reporter: "Do you think it's even possible for Ajax to lose nine points in nine games?"
Zlatan: "According to my calculations it is possible to lose nine points in only three games."

Q: "What are you NOT going to say when you meet your teammates in Ajax for the first time?"
A: "I am Zlatan, who the hell are you?"

"[Jose] Mourinho is [Pep] Guardiola's opposite. If Mourinho brightens up the room, Guardiola pulls down the curtains and I guessed that Guardiola now tried to measure himself with him."

He compares the two big-name managers

"I think this is the best season of my career. I think my league form has been more than perfect."

Zlatan sums up his 2011/12 campaign for AC Milan in the only way he can

Q: "What did you learn from Mido?"

A: "Arabian music!"

"First I went left, he did too. Then I went right, he did too. Then I went left again, and he went to buy a hot dog."

The Swede describes his duel with Liverpool defender Stephane Henchoz

"Come over to my house with your sister, baby, and I'll show you who's gay!"

He was asked by a female journalist about a picture of him and Gerard Pique hugging

Reporter: "What would you name your son?"

Zlatan: "Zlatan Jr."

TV reporter: "But your strength is..."

TV producer: "Excuse me, they say you have to go to training now [for Inter]."

Zlatan: "No, we finish this one. How much time do you have left? Eight minutes? No, no, we finish this one. Training starts when I say so, haha!"

Zlatan does training when Zlatan decides

"The only thing he did that I haven't done – yet – is acting. I'm a little bit curious also to be an actor. Something like Bourne Identity, something like that, a secret agent. The new James Bond – why not?!"

Zlatan would like to be next 007

Zlatan beams with joy after signing for Barcelona in 2009.

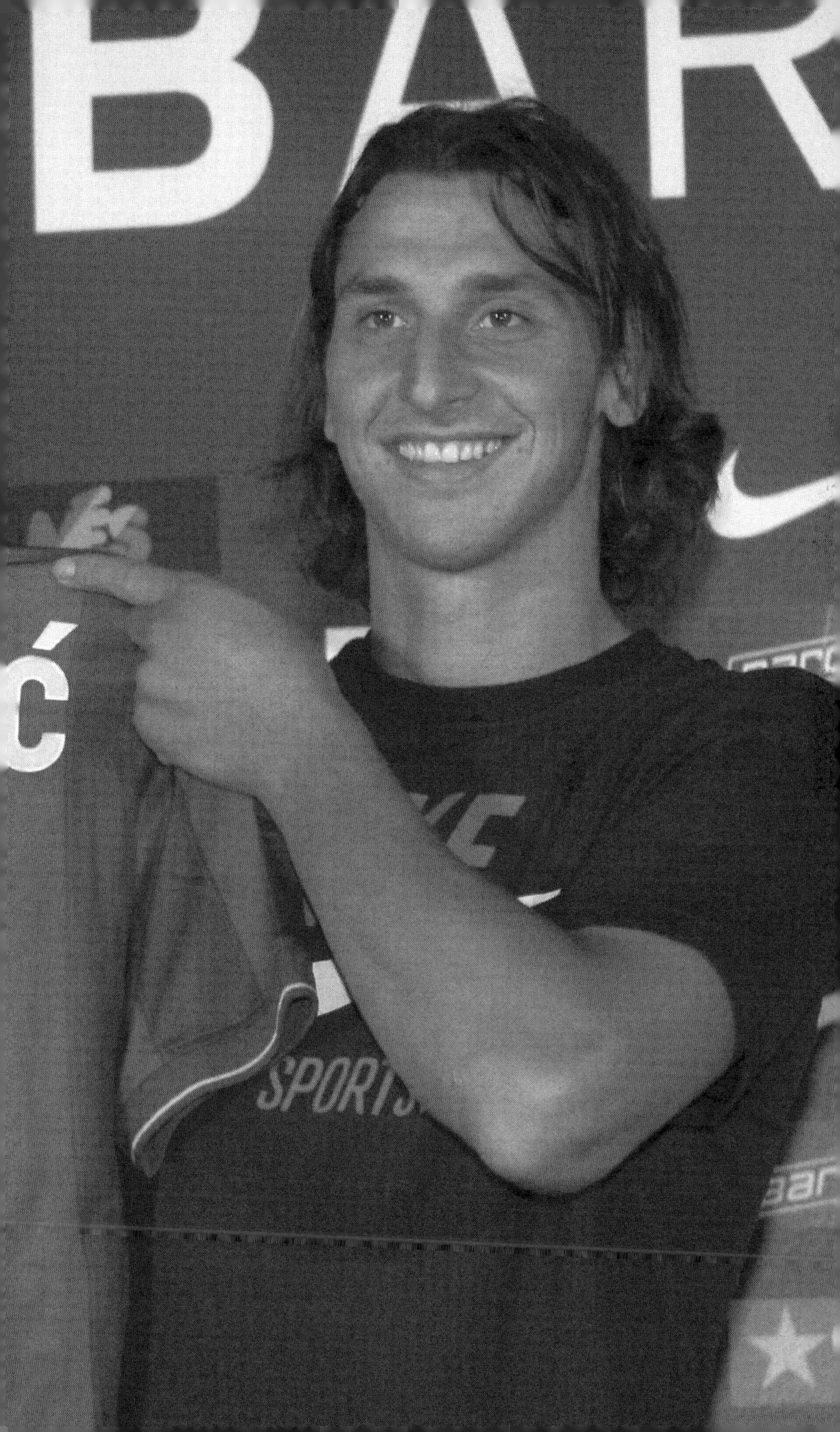

"It was the fault of David Trezeguet, who made me do one drink of vodka after another. I slept in the bathtub. Now I hold my vodka much better."

On having a few too many drinks while celebrating Juventus' 2005 title victory

"If Materazzi had attacked me like that, I would've decked him in a second!"

Zlatan on Marco Materazzi slapping AC Milan teammate Mario Balotelli

Reporter: "Who is the most beautiful woman in the world?"

Zlatan: "I haven't met her yet. But when I do, I'll date her."

"At Barca, players were banned from driving their sports cars to training. I thought this was ridiculous – it was no one's business what car I drive. So in April, before a match with Almeria, I drove my Ferrari Enzo to work. It caused a scene."

Zlatan drives the car Zlatan wants

Zlatan: "Only God knows who will go through."

Reporter: "It's hard to ask him."

Zlatan: "You're talking to him."

It was put to Zlatan who would triumph from the two World Cup play-off games between Sweden and Portugal

"We finished second in our group behind Germany, the best team in Europe. They [Portugal] finished second in a group they should have won. I think we deserve more to go to Brazil."

Zlatan explains who the better side is before Sweden's World Cup play-off match against Portugal

"I am getting better and better, and like I said, I feel like Benjamin Button. I was born old and I will die young!"

Zlatan, 35, compares himself to the movie character who ages in reverse

"It's true that I don't know much about the players in Ligue 1, but for sure, they know who I am."

Speaking on his arrival in France to play for Paris Saint-Germain

"If I'd gone into taekwondo, I'd probably have won several Olympic medals."

The ever-confident Swede attained a black belt in taekwondo as a teenager

"I want to play on so that I can show that 'the legend' can still deliver."

Zlatan to the media ahead of Sweden's Euro 2016 opener against Ireland

"I'm not used to winning nothing – it's the first time it's happened to me. I'm disappointed. It's a failure."

On missing out on the Serie A title with AC Milan in 2012

"With all respect for what the ladies have done, and they've done it fantastically well, you can't compare men's and women's football. Give it up, it's not even funny."

Zlatan believes male footballers deserve more recognition than female players

"I started to adapt and blend in. I became way too nice. I said what I thought people wanted me to say. It was completely messed up. I drove the club's Audi and stood there and nodded my head. I hardly even yelled at my teammates any more. I was boring. Zlatan was no longer Zlatan."

The striker admits he didn't fit in at Barcelona

"Master your man stare. I have mine, make sure you find yours. So then people will be afraid of you."

Zlatan gives tips on how to be like him

Zlatan tries some fancy footwork for Manchester United in a Europa League tie against Zorya Luhansk.

Photo: Maxisport/Shutterstock.com

"I heard Beckham's decision and it made me think. Who is most deserving of all of the money that I, Zlatan, am paid? The answer is Zlatan. The children of Paris are not leading Ligue 1 in goals this season. I am. I have 20 goals. The next best players have 12. 12! If anything, the children of Paris should be giving me even more money for having the privilege of being in the same city as my incredible quality. And so should David Beckham. Call it a Zlaritable donation."

Zlatan will donate all his wages to himself, despite PSG teammate David Beckham announcing he will give his salary to a children's charity in Paris

Reporter: "Just how big a difference does he [Zlatan] make? He's a very modest guy as we know."

Paul Pogba: "That's why we bought him."

Zlatan: "Bought me? I came for free. They bought you."

Reporter: "Do you sense something more special happening here after today?" [United winning the EFL Cup].

Zlatan: "I came – that's special."

"Give them [women footballers] a bicycle with my autograph and that will be enough."

Zlatan believes female players don't deserve the same financial rewards as males

Zlatan: "How you doing?"

Zoumana Camara: "Yeah, I'm OK. You?"

Zlatan: "You're even more ugly on television than real life, haha."

Camara: "And they even put on the make-up, so can you imagine, haha."

PSG defender Zoumana Camara interviews his then-teammate on French television

"I'm only 21 years! Hello, is my name Maradona?"

On criticism faced when the Ajax striker was up against world-class defenders

"Hasse [Borg] keeps telling me I wouldn't have made it if I hadn't met him. But he always brags. I would have made tunnels on him all the time."

Tunnels? Zlatan on the former Malmo FF defender

"I am the greatest! Wait, is that even possible? Alright, then I'm the greatest behind [Muhammad] Ali!"

Zlatan is happy to be no.2 – for once

Q: "If I say Anders Svensson and Kim Kallstrom, what do you say?"

A: "Zlatan."

"I felt like crap when I was sitting in the locker room with Guardiola staring at me like I was an annoying distraction, an outsider. It was nuts. He was a wall, a stone wall. I didn't get any sign of life from him and I was wishing myself away every moment with the team. Then Guardiola started his philosopher thing. I was barely listening. Why would I? It was advanced bullsh*t about blood, sweat and tears, that kind of stuff."

On the management techniques of Pep Guardiola

Q: "Do you have a pet?"

A: "Yes, Joey Didulica!"

Zlatan on his then-Ajax teammate

"I'm number one. I really feel that way. If you think you are the second, it's the end. The fact that I have never won the Ballon d'Or and FIFA World Player doesn't mean that I cannot be number one."

The striker has been overlooked for the top individual honours

"During the World Cup in 2002, I was voted man of the match three times in Sweden, even though I hadn't played. The people love me."

On his limited appearances at the finals in Japan and South Korea

Zlatan controls the ball on his chest for Sweden against France at Euro 2012, in Ukraine.

"Wake up, wake up... We're not amateurs. F*cking asshole. I've never seen this in my 15 years playing football. I've been playing for 15 years and I've never seen [good] refereeing in this sh*t country. They don't even deserve PSG in this country."

Zlatan rages after PSG had just lost 3-2 against Bordeaux

"With a hat-trick there is no better way to start 2014. The standing ovation? It was easy because there were only 500 people in the stands, but yes, I'm happy."

Zlatan was not impressed with his standing ovation after a treble away at Ligue 2's Brest in the French Cup

"I score a lot of goals that are hard to replicate. I don't think that you can score as spectacular a goal as those of Zlatan in a video game – even though these games are very realistic these days."

On recreating his best strikes on games consoles

"When you come to New York, you have the statue of Liberty. When you come to Sweden, you have the statue of Zlatan."

Zlatan compares himself to the Statue of Liberty

"When the red card happened the worst thing was the Chelsea players. I felt there were 11 babies around me."

On being sent off for PSG at Stamford Bridge in the Champions League, in 2015

"If Rooney still wants to move next summer, I would urge him to come and play with me in Paris. But he would have to get used to the fact that Zlatan scores even better goals than him."

When asked about Wayne Rooney's reported move to PSG

"While at Ajax, my friend Mido, who went on to play in the Premier League, declared publicly that he wanted to be transferred. He wasn't exactly a diplomat; he was worse than me. After one match, when he'd been on the bench against Eindhoven, he came into the locker room and called us all miserable c*nts. I responded by saying if anybody was a c*nt, it was him. Mido picked up a pair of scissors and flung them at me. It was completely nuts. The scissors whizzed past my head, straight into the concrete wall and made a crack in it. I went over and gave him a smack, but 10 minutes later we left with our arms around each other."

Zlatan versus Mido

"England is a very strong league, with three or four of the best teams in Europe. But if I had played there, I would have destroyed it, like I have everywhere else. Arsenal could have happened, as everybody knows, but I would not do a trial. Who do you think regrets that more – Arsene Wenger or Zlatan?"

Speaking before he joined Man United, Zlatan had rejected Arsenal because Arsene Wenger wanted him to have a trial first

"That man has no natural authority, no proper charisma. If you didn't know he was the manager of a top team, you'd hardly notice him entering a room."

On Pep Guardiola

"Messi, Xavi, Iniesta, the whole gang – they were like schoolboys. The best footballers in the world stood there with their heads bowed, and I didn't understand any of it. It was ridiculous."

On his Barcelona teammates

Q: "Where do you come up with your moves?"

A: "They just come, I promise. It is nothing that I plan."

"[Steven] Gerrard has good skills, unlike normal English players."

Zlatan takes a swipe at the England side

Zlatan is deeply focused during Paris Saint-German's Champions League tie against Shakhtar Donetsk.

"As for Cristiano Ronaldo, we did not play together. It is different because it is the result of hard training. It is not natural."

Zlatan aims a dig at the Portugal playmaker, suggesting he has no natural talent

"People that know me know that I play in many clubs and I try to do my best. Wherever I went I won, so I am like Indiana Jones."

Comparing himself to the Hollywood star

"I came like a king, left like a legend."

Zlatan on his departure from Paris Saint-Germain

The funniest Zlatan Ibrahimovic quotes!

Journalist: "Is your fitness a natural fitness?"

Zlatan: "I feel fresh. I feel good. I'm an animal. I feel like a lion."

Journalist: "Why are you like a lion?"

Zlatan: "I am a lion. I don't want to be a lion."

Journalist: "Do you mean you have the hunger of a lion?"

Zlatan: "The lion is born a lion."

Journalist: "What does that mean?"

Zlatan: "It means I'm a lion! I never talk so much with journalists. I never stopped so long even for the French people."

Journalist: "You say you've got 32 medals what do you do with them?"

Zlatan: "It is in the museum. I have a house only for the medals."

Reporter: "Zlatan, I see they are building a fantastic statue of you in Sweden. But tonight, can you do the honours for me and just give Paul [Pogba] this man-of-the-match award?"

Zlatan: "No, I will keep it for me, haha."

The Swede in good spirits after United's win over Crystal Palace

"It's good that Balotelli compares himself to me, because I don't compare myself to him."

Zlatan responds to Mario Balotelli's quote: "Comparing me to Ibrahimovic is a compliment to him"

"In [Malmo] MBI, the Swedish dads stood and yelled, 'Come on, guys. Good work!' In [FBK] Balkan it was more, 'I will f*ck your mother up the ass'. They were crazy Yugoslavs who smoked a lot and threw shoes around them and I thought, 'Wonderful, exactly like home. I belong here!'"

Zlatan played for different youth sides but felt more comfortable at FBK Balkan

"As a coach, he was fantastic. As a person, I've no comments about that, that's something else. He's not a man, there's nothing more to say."

Zlatan on Pep Guardiola

"I don't give a sh*t about ethnic crap, and seriously, how could I? We're a mess in my family. Dad's a Bosnian, mum from Croatia, and the little brother has a dad who's a Serb."

Zlatan blasts a reporter who billed a clash between him and the Serbian Inter Milan defender Sinisa Mihajlovic as a 'Balkan War'

Zlatan: "Have you ever done an interview before?"

Journalist: "I've never interviewed you before."

Zlatan: "Don't be nervous."

"I've travelled around like Napoleon and conquered every new country where I've set foot. So perhaps I should do what Napoleon didn't and cross the Atlantic and conquer the States as well."

Zlatan considers playing in the USA

"I like guys who drive through red lights. I always drive like a maniac. I've done 325 kmph in my Porsche Turbo and left the cops eating my dust. I've done so much mental stuff I don't even want to think about it."

Zlatan the adrenaline junkie

Zlatan keeps his eye on the ball for Inter Milan.

"I took the opportunity to take a selfie with myself at the Grevin Museum in Paris. The one to the right is made of wax and the one to the left is made of steel."

Zlatan poses for a selfie with the wax version of himself

Fan on Twitter: "Is Zlatan human? Or should he be worshipped like a God?"

Zlatan tweets back: "Yes. Zlatan is just a human. The same way a great white shark is just a fish."

"When I signed with PSG, the politicians called my wages 'indecent' in a time when so many people are struggling, even though it is a lot of money that can be taxed and help the country. Now Beckham gives all of his wages to a local charity and people call him a tax dodger. Both are examples of stupid people complaining about good things. It is a waste of breath. Like Pep Guardiola blowing up his own birthday balloons, which I then pop with an overhead kick the second he is finished. These people should be subject to a 75 per cent stupidity tax payable to the Bank of Zlatan. Then they will have something to really complain about."

Zlatan on his Paris Saint-Germain salary

Journalist: "Zlatan, this is your first goal in the league for two months, you feel better now?"

Zlatan: "For two months?"

Journalist: "Yes, in the league, Ligue 1."

Zlatan: "And Saint-Etienne? [Where he had scored]. Please my friend. If you don't know your information, don't talk to me."

Zlatan walks out of the mixed zone after a reporter gets his facts wrong following a 1-1 draw with Lyon

"You can take the boy out of the ghetto, but you can never take the ghetto out of the boy."

The Swede grew up in a tough part of Malmo

"Do you think that you are my mother?"

Zlatan to Malmo FF coach Michael Andersson during training

Reporter: "How many one night stands have you had in total?"

Zlatan: "I don't do that stuff. For me it is romance and love… right?"

"What [John] Carew does with a football, I can do with an orange."

On the former Aston Villa striker John Carew who criticised him for his "pointless" skills

Journalist: "A lot of people speak about your relationship with Edinson [Cavani]..."

Zlatan: "A lot of people or you?"

Journalist: "A lot of press people."

Zlatan: "A lot of people or you?"

Journalist: "I speak sometimes about your relationship. What is the real relationship between you and him?"

Zlatan: "But you seem to know better than me."

Journalist: "No, no, I don't know..."

Zlatan: "But you are writing about it, not me."

Journalist: "I'm waiting for you. I'd like to know..."

Zlatan: "But still you are talking about it, so how do you know?"

Journalist: "How do we know? We know that you have scored a lot of goals since you arrived... But sometimes you should have a better relationship... Even the coach says that."

Zlatan: "And you know football better than me?"

Journalist: "No."

Zlatan: "So why are you talking?"

Journalist: "I ask you. I'm doing my job."

Zlatan: "Are you a journalist or a camera guy?"

Journalist: "I am a journalist."

Zlatan: "So why are you holding the camera? You should have a camera guy, no?"

Journalist: "Because my boss wants me to..."

Zlatan: [Smiles] "So it's low budget?"

Journalist: "But you don't want to answer?"

Zlatan: "I answer you. The relationship is perfect. You are dependent on the team and when the team is doing good, we are doing good. So that's your answer."

The mixed zone after PSG's win over Rennes

Zlatan is shown the red card for AC Milan in their clash with Napoli at the San Siro.

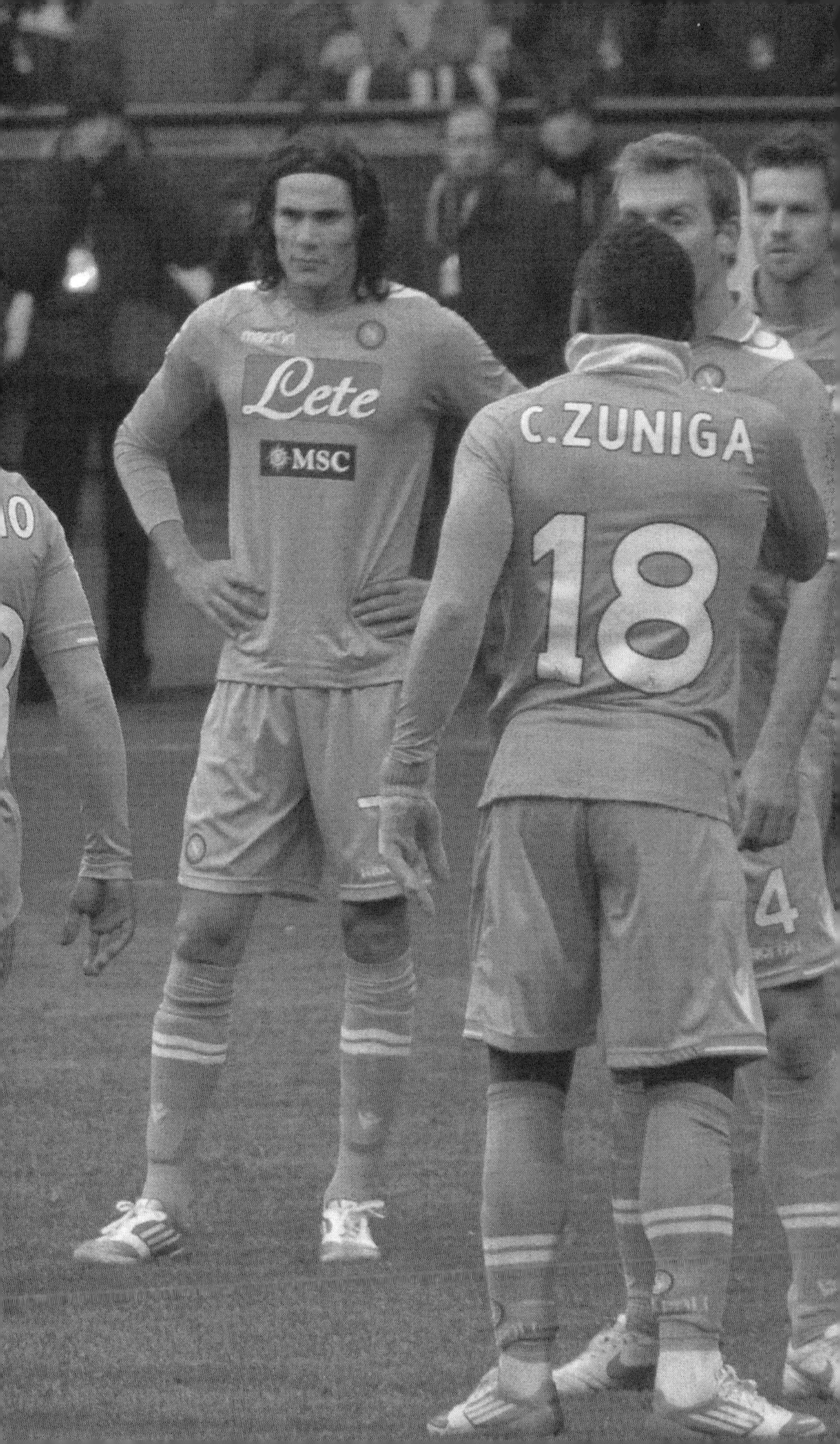
Lete
MSC
C.ZUNIGA
18

Q: "Which other sportsman would you compare yourself to?"

A: "I'm like Muhammed Ali. When he said he would knock someone out in the fourth round, he did it."

"That's how it is with the English: if you score against them you're a good player; if you don't, you're not."

The Swedish striker on his wonder goal against England

"There's only one Zlatan."

Perfectly summed up after Ajax's match against NAC where he scored a hat-trick

"I am disappointed by the boos. We played well, we won. We don't understand what these guys want. Whether we win or we lose, they boo us. Maybe they are in the habit of eating caviar before they come to see us."
Zlatan's 'prawn-sandwich brigade' quip about the Paris fans after their win over Rennes

"What is this? Remember I'm only 20 years old."
When asked about the time Sweden's Magnus Hedman dropped his pants to get a pain-killing injection against Senegal in the World Cup

Q: "Did time stop as you stood waiting on the touchline to come on against Argentina in the World Cup?"

A: "You could have punched me in the face, I wouldn't have noticed."

"I yelled to him, 'You have no balls!' And probably worse things than that. And I added, 'You are sh*tting yourself about Mourinho! You can go to hell!' I was completely mad."

He blasts his then-Barcelona manager Pep Guardiola

"If you don't stop that, I'll put you in that f*cking bin!"

Zlatan warns AC Milan teammate Gennaro Gattuso who was throwing grapes at him, before he threw the Italian to the floor when he refused to stop

"Nobody should know I exist. Then when we're back, I'll strike down on the pitch like a bolt of lightning."

Zlatan after Malmo had been relegated from the Swedish first division

ZLATAN STYLE

Others...
on Zlatan

"At the start of the season, he asked me how many goals I'd scored during my loan spell at Valenciennes. I told him I'd scored two goals in 21 matches. And he replied, with his accent: 'Pfff, and you think that's good? Bahebeck: two goals, 21 matches. With Zlatan it's two matches, 21 goals!"

PSG striker Jean-Christophe Bahebeck

"Zlatan is the best known Swede in the world – he is even more famous than IKEA!"

Tennis great Bjorn Borg

"With him, even the referees sh*t themselves."

TV pundit and ex-France star Basile Boli

"I have had the desire to throw a punch at Ibrahimovic more than once. We have said things to each other in English that I can't repeat in public. He is playing a role with his arrogant behaviour and he is doing it very well. They should give him an Oscar for it."

Marseille forward Rod Fanni

"Zlatan is unique – he's the only player in the world who measures 1.96 metres, has the technique of Lionel Messi, the character of Muhammad Ali, and the strength of Mike Tyson."

Zlatan's agent Mino Raiola

"He called me an English so-and-so, so I replied, 'Yeah, I'm English, but you've got a huge nose' and I did the gesture showing his huge nose."
Marseille midfielder Joey Barton on his clash with the PSG forward

"He is the kind of chest-puffing player, who is arrogant."
Fenerbahce defender Simon Kjaer

"Perhaps you could ask Ibra for an interview. I'm sure he'd grant you one."
PSG manager Laurent Blanc to a TV reporter after Zlatan gatecrashes her interview with him

"Ibrahimovic is so big-headed. People make him think he's intelligent, but he's as thick as two short planks. He's not a caricature, but he's not far off. He's an out-and-out bully. If PSG want to progress they need to get rid of him. You can't ask him to accept playing upfront alongside someone because he's too stupid."

Former France goalkeeper Jean-Paul Bertrand-Demanes

"Zlatan, three words: he's a winner, he's a goalscorer, and he's funny – he's a funny guy."

Manchester United boss Jose Mourinho

Zlatan warms up with
pre-match free-kicks for
Paris Saint-Germain.

"Zlatan's the best. We used to sleep in the same room before games. One night, he woke up. Ibra told me, 'Adi, wake up! I had a nightmare. I dreamed Ronaldo was better than me!' He only went back to sleep after I told him, 'No, Zlatan, no! You are the best in the world! Calm down!'"

Adrian Mutu on his ex-Juventus teammate

"I've been at this school for 33 years and he is easily in the top five most unruly pupils we have ever had."

Agneta Cederbom, Zlatan's headmistress at Sorgenfriskolan school

"There was a problem during the match. At one point, the Freebox [satellite box] wasn't sending the right signal. Zlatan took the remote control and showed what you had to do to watch the match properly. He's a handyman!"

A Paris restaurant owner recalls the moment Zlatan fixed his TV while the PSG squad watched a Champions League tie between Barcelona and Milan

"You're going to sell your cars. You're going to sell your watches and start training three times harder. Because your stats are crap."

Zlatan's agent Mino Raiola motivates the then-Ajax player

"After a perfectly normal challenge, Ibra turned to me and provoked me, making a joke about my moustache, saying, 'That really is terrible'. I responded by saying that he should think about his nose."

Anderlecht midfielder Sacha Kljestan

"Ibra is a strong personality and needs to be relaxed at times, while in other occasions he has to be stimulated, otherwise he falls asleep."

Milan coach Massimiliano Allegri on his task to keep Zlatan awake

"Ibrahimovic used his book to explain what he believes, he had some things to say. Always I was clear. Whatever I said to him I spoke face to face. I never used the media to explain what I wanted from him on the pitch."

Pep Guardiola

"Before winning the 2012/13 league title, we were getting ready to play against Lyon. Carlo Ancelotti was a bit tense, so Ibra approached him and asked him if he believed in Jesus. Ancelotti said, 'Yes'. So Ibra told him, 'Good, so you believe in me. You can relax!'"

PSG midfielder Marco Verratti

"We need a ladder to stop a player like Zlatan Ibrahimovic because he's so tall."

Barcelona manager Pep Guardiola on the aerial threat of AC Milan's Zlatan

Leo Beenhakker: "If you f*ck me, I f*ck you."
The Ajax technical director's words to Zlatan after he signed for the Dutch giants. The striker replied: "No worries – I'll not f*ck you. I'll make it happen"

"We wanted to give the dog a special name, and we all liked the name 'Ibra' a lot."

Midfielder Mark van Bommel on his mutt

"It's no use people turning up for work like Eeyore the donkey. Sure, Eeyore is a good friend. But he's always sad and walks around with his head down. I would much rather my players were like Winnie the Pooh, who is bright and cheerful and believes anything is possible."

Sweden coach Erik Hamren on luring Zlatan out of international retirement

"The problem is that he's got people used to caviar. On Wednesday, he only served smoked salmon."

Gerard Houllier on Zlatan's disappointing display for PSG against Chelsea in the Champions League, in 2014

Zlatan in action for Sweden at Euro 2004, in France.

ZLATAN STYLE

Zlatan fact file

ZLATAN STYLE

Full name: Zlatan Ibrahimovic.

Nationality: Swedish.

1981: Born in Malmo on 3rd October. Zlatan Ibrahimovic grows up in the Swedish city and begins playing for local junior sides Malmo BI and FBK Balkan.

1994: Aged 13, he joins senior club Malmo FF and signs his first contract two years later.

1999: Zlatan progresses to the first team, but Malmo finish 13th and are relegated to the second tier for the first time in their history.

2000: As the club's leading scorer, his goals help Malmo bounce back to the top division.

2001: Makes his international debut for Sweden against the Faroe Islands on 31st January. His sparkling displays catch the attention of a number of clubs, and on 22nd March, Zlatan is transferred to Ajax for a Swedish record fee of €8.7m. The 19-year-old doesn't get much game time, but that changes with the arrival of new manager Ronald Koeman in November.

2002: Zlatan clinches the first of many championships when Ajax win the 2001/02 Eredivisie title, plus the KNVB Cup and Johan Cruyff Shield. Plays for Sweden at the 2002 FIFA World Cup, in Japan and South Korea.

2003: He scores five Champions League goals as Ajax progress to the quarter-finals before they are knocked out by AC Milan. Domestically, Ajax finish runners-up in the Eredivisie.

2004: In Zlatan's last season at the club, Ajax win back the Dutch title. He represents Sweden at Euro 2004, in Portugal. In August, Zlatan injures Ajax teammate Rafael van der Vaart in a clash during Sweden's match with Holland which the Dutchman feels was deliberate. It leads to Zlatan abruptly being sold to Juventus on 31st August for €16m.

2005: Zlatan finishes as Juve's top scorer as they secure the Serie A title. He is announced as Serie A Foreign Footballer of the Year.

2006: The Old Lady repeat the feat with another

Scudetto the following campaign. However, Juve are stripped of their last two titles as part of a football corruption scandal and are demoted to Serie B. Zlatan travels with Sweden to Germany for the 2006 World Cup. On his return, he joins boyhood club Inter Milan for €24.8m on 10th August and then wins the Supercoppa Italiana.

2007: Zlatan helps I Nerazzurri capture the Serie A title in his first season.

2008: The striker is the top goal scorer as Inter retain the Scudetto and also the Supercoppa Italiana. He is named both Serie A Footballer of the Year and Serie A Foreign Footballer of the Year for 2007/08. Plays for Sweden in Euro 2008, held in Austria and Switzerland.

2009: He makes it a third straight title success for Inter and finishes as the division's top scorer. Wins Footballer of the Year and Foreign Footballer of the Year again. Zlatan's exploits grab the attention of Spanish giants Barcelona who swoop in deal worth €69.5m on 29th July. Barca clinch the Supercopa de Espana and the FIFA Club World Cup.

2010: More silverware is claimed with Barcelona winning the 2009/10 La Liga title and the UEFA Super Cup. Zlatan wins the Supercopa de Espana at the start of the next season but his strained relationship with coach Pep Guardiola leads to him departing the Catalan club. And on 28th August, the Swede joins AC Milan on a season-long loan.

2011: Zlatan ends the campaign as Milan's top scorer as they claim the Serie A crown. He is named Serie A Footballer of the Year. Milan take out their option to buy Zlatan for €24m and the 2011 Supercoppa Italiana is next in the trophy bag for him.

2012: Milan are Serie A runners-up and Zlatan is the league's leading scorer. On 18th July, the striker goes on the move to France where he joins Paris Saint-Germain for €20m. He then heads out to Ukraine with the Sweden squad to play at Euro 2012. Back in club competition, Zlatan becomes the first man to score for six different clubs in the UEFA Champions League when he nets in PSG's match against Dynamo Kyiv in September.

2013: He caps a memorable maiden season by winning the Ligue 1 title to go with the division's player of the year and leading scorer accolades. The Trophee des Champions is added to his trophy haul.

2014: Helps PSG to another Ligue 1 title plus the Coupe de la Ligue, and again he ends the campaign by winning Ligue 1's Player of the Year award and the league's top scorer honour. He scores in the 2014 Trophee des Champions victory. On 4th September, Zlatan notches his 50th goal for Sweden to become his country's highest-ever goal scorer.

2015: Zlatan secures another Ligue 1 as PSG also help themselves to the Coupe de la Ligue and Coupe de France. Becomes PSG's all-time leading scorer with 110 goals in October, before claiming another Trophee des Champions.

2016: It's yet another domestic cup treble for PSG, including the Ligue 1 title for the fourth time. Zlatan is also the league's player of the year and top scorer for the third time each. Plays for Sweden at Euro 2016, in France, and retires from international football after their exit on 22nd June after a record 62 goals from 116 games. Makes his move to Manchester United on a free transfer on 1st July. Scores the winner in the Red Devils' FA Community Shield victory.

2017: Scores twice, including the winner, in United's EFL Cup triumph over Southampton.

Zlatan shares a joke during training with Barcelona.

Photo: Christian Bertrand/Shutterstock.com

10 Facts on Zlatan

1) Zlatan Ibrahimovic was born in Sweden to a Bosnian father and a Croatian mother, who both emigrated to Sweden where they met.

2) He has two sons – Maximilian and Vincent – with former TV presenter and actress/model Helena Seger.

3) A song dedicated to him called, 'Who's Da Man' stayed at the top of the Swedish charts for 10 weeks in 2006.

4) At 17, Zlatan got a black belt in Taekwondo. He also received an honorary black belt from the Italian Taekwondo Federation.

5) He is fluent in his native language Swedish, plus Bosnian, English, Spanish and Italian.

6) The ex-PSG star has a special burger named after him in a Paris cafe called 'Le Zlatan'.

7) Sweden issued a set of five unique postal stamps on him in 2014.

8) The word "Zlatan" is trademarked and the term "To Zlatan" is in the Swedish dictionary.

9) The striker has the highest combined transfer fee total in football history at €171m.

10) He has won the Swedish Footballer of the Year award a record-breaking nine times.

Playing career

Youth team

Malmo BI, FBK Balkan, Malmo FF.

Senior team

1999–2001   Malmo FF.

2001–2004   Ajax.

2004–2006   Juventus.

2006–2009   Inter Milan.

2009–2011   Barcelona.

2010–2012   AC Milan.

2012–2016   Paris Saint-Germain.

2016–   Manchester United.

International team

2001–2016   Sweden.

Club honours

Ajax

Eredivisie: 2001/02, 2003/04.

KNVB Cup: 2001/02.

Johan Cruyff Shield: 2002.

Juventus

Serie A: 2004/05, 2005/06 (both invalidated due to the Calciopoli scandal).

Inter Milan

Serie A: 2006/07, 2007/08, 2008/09.

Supercoppa Italiana: 2006, 2008.

Barcelona

La Liga: 2009/10.

Supercopa de Espana: 2009, 2010.

UEFA Super Cup: 2009.

FIFA Club World Cup: 2009.

AC Milan

Serie A: 2010/11.

Supercoppa Italiana: 2011.

Paris Saint-Germain

Ligue 1: 2012/13, 2013/14, 2014/15, 2015/16.

Coupe de France: 2014/15, 2015/16.

Coupe de la Ligue: 2013/14, 2014/15, 2015/16.

Trophee des Champions: 2013, 2014, 2015.

Manchester United

EFL Cup: 2016/17.

Individual honours

Serie A Foreign Footballer of the Year: 2005, 2008, 2009.

Serie A Footballer of the Year: 2008, 2009, 2011.

Serie A Team of the Year: 2010/11, 2011/12.

Serie A Top Scorer: 2009, 2012.

UEFA Team of the Year: 2007, 2009, 2013, 2014.

UEFA Champions League Team of the Season: 2013/14.

Ligue 1 Player of the Year: 2012/13, 2013/14, 2015/16.

Ligue 1 Team of the Year: 2012/13, 2013/14, 2014/15, 2015/16.

Ligue 1 Top scorer: 2012/13, 2013/14, 2015/16.

Zlatan alongside his Paris
Saint-Germain teammate
Thiago Silva.

ZLATAN STYLE

Printed in Great
Britain
by Amazon